HOW DO WE APPLY SCIENCE?

THINK LIKE A SCIENTIST

by Dru Hunter

CREATIVE EDUCATION • CREATIVE PAPERBACKS

Published by **Creative Education** and **Creative Paperbacks**
P.O. Box 227, Mankato, Minnesota 56002
Creative Education and Creative Paperbacks are imprints of The Creative Company
www.thecreativecompany.us

Design and production by **Christine Vanderbeek**
Art direction by **Rita Marshall**
Printed in Malaysia

Photographs by Corbis (AMELIE-BENOIST/BSIP, Bettmann, Ron Boardman/
Frank Lane Picture Agency, Corbis, Stephen Frink, Mark Garlick/Science Photo
Library, GraphicaArtis, Steven Hobbs/Stocktrek Images, Wilfredo Lee, Michael
Nicholson, Vincent Parker/U.S. Air Force/epa, Roger Ressmeyer, Science Photo
Library, Stocktrek Images, Sunset Boulevard, Eric Tschaen/epa, VICTOR HABBICK
VISIONS/Science Photo Library, Horacio Villalobos/epa), Getty Images (Mat
Hayward, Nathan Lazarnick/George Eastman House), iStockphoto (Guntars
Grebezs, imgendesign, thelinke), NASA (Franklin Fitzgerald), Shutterstock (arka38,
Eugene Berman, Edw, Georgios Kollidas, NatalieJean, Olga Popova, Marina Sun,
ThomasLENNE, VanderWolf Images)

Library of Congress Cataloging-in-Publication Data
Hunter, Dru.
How do we apply science? / Dru Hunter.
p. cm. — (Think like a scientist)
Includes bibliographical references and index.
Summary: A narration of the origins, advancements, and future of the applied
sciences, including engineering and medicine, and the ways in which scientists
utilize the scientific method to explore questions.

ISBN 978-1-60818-592-4 (hardcover)
ISBN 978-1-62832-197-5 (pbk)
1. Science—Methodology—Juvenile literature. 2. Scientists—Juvenile literature.
3. Technology—History—Juvenile literature. I. Title.

Q175.2.H865 2015
500—dc23   2014029751

CCSS: RI.5.1, 2, 3, 8; RI.6.1, 3, 7; RST.6-8.1, 2, 5, 6, 8

First Edition HC 9 8 7 6 5 4 3 2 1
First Edition PBK 9 8 7 6 5 4 3 2 1

ON THE COVER Artistic rendering of Tesla coils firing, showing
electricity's power

TABLE OF CONTENTS

SCIENTIST IN THE SPOTLIGHT

INTRODUCTION

With a flip of a coin, Orville and Wilbur Wright had decided who would be the first to fly their latest invention. In their Ohio bicycle shop, the brothers had built an engine like no other. It was both light and powerful.

They chose the Kill Devil Hills at Kitty Hawk, North Carolina, to test their flying machine because the winds there would help lift the wings—and the sandy beaches would soften the blow if they crashed. Starting the engine, Wilbur pulled sharply on the controls, and the plane lifted. Then it sputtered and stalled, crashing onto the beach. It took three days to fix the craft. Orville's turn came on December 17, 1903. The wind blew at 27 miles (43.5 km) per hour from the north as Orville ran the propeller and engine. Releasing the restraining wire at 10:35 A.M., Orville increased the speed, and the plane lifted into the air. Orville flew the plane for about 120 feet (36.6 m) in 12 seconds. With this first controlled, powered flight, the Wright brothers changed the world, and they did it with applied science.

Applied science answers the question of how something will get done. By investigating nature to discover its inner workings, observing for understanding, and experimenting with one's findings, scientists can develop technologies and invent gadgets to address the problems and dilemmas of everyday life. From the Wright brothers' airplane and other engineering marvels to advances in medicine, computers, fisheries, food, nuclear energy, and crime-solving, all these fields rely on applied science.

REVOLUTIONARY EARLY APPLIED SCIENCE

AT THE CORE OF ALL APPLIED SCIENCE IS THE **scientific method**, which helps scientists gather information and examine what is found. The scientific method is based on asking questions and then trying to answer them with the evidence at hand. There must be sufficient proof to support the answers. Like other applied sciences, the field of forensic science depends on the use of the scientific method.

In ancient times, law enforcement relied on forced confessions or the words of witnesses to prove a crime had occurred. This often meant that criminals went free or innocent people were punished. One of the first written accounts of using forensic science to support a criminal case comes from a Chinese book in A.D. 1248. A Chinese investigator **hypothesized** the weapon used to murder the victim was a sickle and proposed to prove it by testing

Today's police officers use a variety of tools and tech to investigate crime scenes.

different weapons on an animal carcass. He then had everyone from the village meet him with their sickles. The investigator observed that flies had gathered on one particular blade because it had remnants of blood on it. Realizing he had been caught, the murderer confessed.

We've come a long way since then in all the applied sciences, including forensic science, largely thanks to technology. Forensic scientists today can do computerized facial reconstructions to help determine the identity of a skeleton, for instance. And **DNA fingerprinting** reveals whether DNA found at the scene of a crime is from a certain person. Whether science is used to make sure justice is served or to engineer a car that can fly, applied scientists over the course of human history have made many revolutionary inventions that have improved our lives, going all the way back to the invention of the wheel.

The concept of using round wheels to move people and objects was first applied around 3500 B.C. Before that time, transportation options were limited. A desire to get from place to place with greater speed, coupled with the need to carry goods and trade with others, led to the invention of the wheel. Such a will and sense of purpose is always behind innovation. A similar scenario played out with the invention of paper.

Paper was invented by the Chinese around the 2nd century B.C. and was first used for wrapping and protecting objects. Paper used for writing came later and was made from a combination of materials such as mulberry bark and hemp. Pounding the plant fibers and letting the water drain out created a lightweight writing surface. Paper is why we know a lot about and have proof of what happened in early times. For instance, early writings on paper helped us learn about the invention of the compass.

From the first stone wheel (below) to DNA fingerprinting (opposite), applied science has seen much progress.

THOMAS EDISON

Thomas Edison (1847–1931) was born in Ohio as the youngest of seven children. He lived in an era where there were no light bulbs, microphones, or even movies. An attack of the dangerous childhood disease scarlet fever left him nearly deaf, and after attending school for only a few months, Edison completed his education at home. Edison loved to experiment and turned the cellar into his laboratory, always asking questions: *What will happen? Why does it do that? How does that work?* To fund his experiments, he took jobs such as working as a newsboy and selling candy on the Grand Trunk Railway. His first **patent** was for the electric vote recorder in 1868. He later worked on power stations, set up his lab in Menlo Park, New Jersey, and founded the company General Electric. He failed many times over and yet never gave up. In all, Edison patented 1,093 inventions.

Early sailors navigated by staying in sight of land, understanding winds, and examining the stars. Unable to navigate far out at sea under certain weather conditions, they did not travel far. The Chinese invented the magnetic compass around 200 B.C. but did not put it into navigational use until the 1100s. It was made of lodestone, a natural rock that, when suspended, points toward the North and South Poles. Compass technology eventually passed to other sailors around the world. Compasses made it possible for ships to travel more safely the farther from land they ventured. This increased trade and led to a period known as the Age of Discovery (1400s–1600s A.D.), a time when sailors such as Christopher Columbus began exploring the oceans, looking for new trade routes and partners.

Around A.D. 1440, German printer Johannes Gutenberg invented a mechanical printing press because he saw a need for producing metal moveable type to make large quantities of books. Before his invention, making a book was a far more labor-intensive process. Only about 50 pages could be printed a day using wood blocks pressed onto paper. Gutenberg created his printing press by supplementing the existing wood-block printing technology with his own inventions. With moveable metal pieces capable of printing thousands of pages a day—and on both sides of the page—it made it much faster to print and distribute information.

The screw press Gutenberg used descended from the technology of the Romans.

By 1500, the Gutenberg printing press led to the production of more than 20 million books in western Europe. The printing press put more Bibles in people's hands, allowing Christians to read the book for themselves. As a result, commentaries on religious life sprang up, including the Catholic priest Martin Luther's historic 95 Theses, which were written in Latin and spurred the Protestant

DID YOU KNOW? An 1894 black-and-white silent film of a man sneezing was the first American patented motion picture made by Thomas Edison's company. (Prints of individual frames of the film are shown here.)

Reformation. Many historians say the printing press also led to the scientific revolution of the 1500s through 1700s because mass printing made it possible to share knowledge in the emerging modern sciences of math, physics, astronomy, chemistry, biology, and medicine.

In the meantime, inventors returned to the wheel and instead looked for ways to make transportation more powerful and faster. The invention of heat engines ushered in the Industrial Revolution, when engine-powered machines were mass-produced to take people farther and faster than ever before. Early engineers developed external combustion engines such as the steam engine and internal combustion engines powered by fuel such as gasoline. German engineer Karl Benz's 1885 Motorwagen is credited by many as being the first automobile. It ran on an internal combustion engine he designed. In this type of engine, a chemical reaction takes place when a fuel combines with an expanding gas (such as oxygen), which then moves a piston. American businessman Henry Ford improved the car production process, decreasing the price and making it possible for many people to own a car. As transportation improved in the 19th century, inventions were also changing the ways humans communicated with one another.

In 1876, Scottish-born scientist Alexander Graham Bell was awarded a patent for his telephone. Bell's experience with deaf people in his own family led to his experimentation with hearing devices, which in turn led to his invention of the telephone, or electrical speech machine, as he called it. Bell's most famous invention and the improvements made to it since have enabled businesses and individuals worldwide to communicate instantaneously.

Also during the 1800s, several scientists played roles in the invention of **incandescent** lights. However, American inventor Thomas Edison is given credit because he developed a complete light system

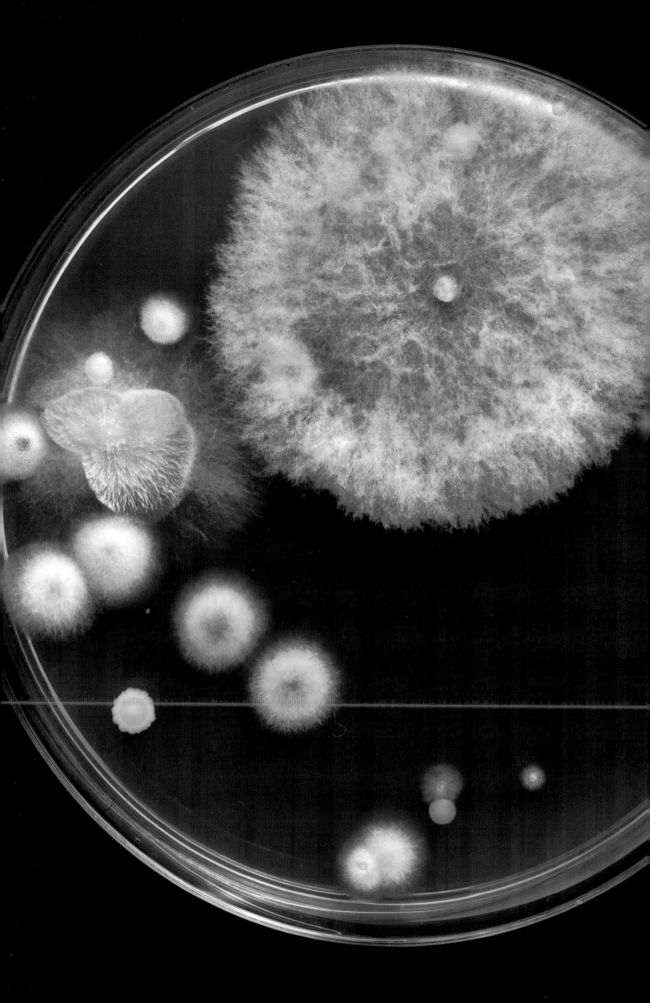

with a generator, bulb, and wiring. Having lights at night meant more work could be done in the evening. Scientists could work even longer on their experiments—and maybe even make world-changing discoveries by accident.

In 1928, Scottish biologist Alexander Fleming returned to his laboratory from vacation and noticed one of his bacteria-filled dishes had the lid open. His specimen had been contaminated by a mold, which had killed the bacteria. Fleming named the bacteria-killing substance penicillin because the mold was from a type of fungus called *Penicillium*. After decades of researching and refining the fungus, the antibiotic penicillin was developed to fight off many human bacterial infections without hurting the person taking it. Not only can applied science find cures to medical ailments, but it can also solve problems with food supplies.

Fishing was vital to early American settlers because it provided employment and food until the land was ready to grow crops. By the 1800s, some of the fish that people had depended on for food had declined to disturbingly low numbers. Fisheries science research began in the 1940s to manage and learn about all the living things people harvest from the water. A fisheries scientist uses his or her scientific knowledge to address needs or problems related to environmental disasters, fish hatcheries, and packaging fish for safe human consumption. As fisheries research began to improve the food supply, though, a war had begun for control of the world.

Innovations may begin with chance fungal formations (opposite) but end in rigorous testing, as with the light bulb (above).

TRY IT OUT! Make a flipbook movie: 1. Get a notepad or stack of Post-its. 2. Draw what you want to see move, such as stick people, on the last page. 3. Sketch the same picture somewhere on the previous page until each page is drawn. 4. Flip the pages and watch your movie!

APPLIED SCIENCE ENDS WAR

N 1939, WORLD WAR II STARTED WHEN GERMANY INVADED Poland. France and Great Britain came to Poland's aid. Because of previous political agreements, the great powers of the world soon formed two sides: the Allies supported Poland and the Axis nations Germany. The United States stayed out of the war until December 7, 1941, "a date which will live in infamy," in the words of then president Franklin D. Roosevelt.

At 7:55 A.M., more than 180 Japanese planes attacked the American base at Pearl Harbor on the Hawaiian island of Oahu. A Marine base adjacent to Pearl Harbor was also targeted, and within five minutes, the sky was overrun with Japanese bombers raining torpedoes on the U.S. warships in the harbor. The 110-minute assault sank 6 U.S. ships, greatly damaged 12, destroyed the naval bases, and killed more than 2,300. News of the event shocked the American people,

Bombed battleships such as the West Virginia *were beyond saving at Pearl Harbor.*

and the U.S. declared war on Japan the next day.

The applied science used to develop weapons on both sides was a level playing field. Both the Axis and the Allied powers had similar aircraft, warships, and guns, but the discovery of atomic power would soon set scientists on each side racing against each other.

An atom is the basic unit of every chemical element. At the center of an atom is a positively charged nucleus made of **protons** and **neutrons**. In the late 1930s, some scientists thought a big, powerful explosion might be possible if an atom of certain chemical elements such as uranium could be split. They hypothesized that one bomb made up of splitting atoms could level entire cities. The scientist who set such theories in motion was Albert Einstein, a German physicist who had immigrated to the U.S. in 1933 because his life was endangered by anti-Jewish attitudes that had reached a fever pitch. Concerned that Germany would develop an atomic bomb and cause irreparable damage, Einstein wrote to President Roosevelt. The president organized a team of scientists to study the issue in October 1939.

Code-named the Manhattan Project, the program employed the talents and minds of some of America's leading scientists. They applied their cumulative knowledge of physics, chemistry, and math to engineer the bomb. Harnessing atomic, or nuclear, power was difficult. First, the power had to be created through fission, the splitting of an atom's nucleus, or core. Then the fission chain reaction had to be controlled to produce a more stable form of energy. It required uranium, the heaviest natural element on Earth, which has 92 protons and 143 neutrons. Italian-American physicist Enrico Fermi discovered that neutrons could break apart atoms. He used Einstein's equation $E=mc^2$ as the mathematical basis for theorizing that nuclear fission would result in the release of never-before-imagined energy.

The Bohr model, showing electrons orbiting a tightly packed nucleus, provides a basic intro to atomic structure.

MARTHA COSTON

Martha Coston (1826–1904) married an inventor but was widowed with 4 children at the age of 21. In an effort to support the family, she continued her husband's work on the development of a signal flare. With the help of chemists and fireworks experts, Martha spent years observing fireworks displays and experimenting with designs. She was finally granted a patent (in her husband's name) for Pyrotechnic Night Signals in 1859. The U.S. Navy paid her $20,000 in 1861 for the rights to use her flares and had her manufacture them. Coston flares were used by the navy in ship-to-ship communication and in signaling to shore. After the Civil War, Martha invented a twist ignition device and took out another patent on the flares. She sold her flares internationally, and they are still used by the U.S. Navy (as shown above) and other groups today.

The *E* in Einstein's statement stood for energy, the *m* for mass, and *c* for the speed of light (squared, or multiplied by itself). The more matter one has, the more energy is created. Uranium has a lot of proton and neutron matter, and when one of the atoms splits, it loses mass. Even though the atom is small, it creates a tremendous amount of energy. Through observation and testing, Fermi and his team of scientists were able to find out that, when they split uranium atoms, stray neutrons would hit other atoms of uranium. Controlling the atoms as the neutrons split other nuclei made for a safe source of nuclear power. An uncontrolled reaction would destroy everything around it. In December 1942, Fermi directed the first controlled nuclear chain reaction, and the Manhattan Project leapt forward.

As the nuclear bomb became a reality, more money and people were assigned to work on it. J. Robert Oppenheimer, a chemist and physicist, was the director of the Manhattan Project and Los Alamos, a secret laboratory in northern New Mexico set up for researching the development of nuclear weapons. Fermi and the other scientists worked with Oppenheimer on developing a uranium bomb nicknamed "Little Boy" and a plutonium bomb called simply "The Gadget." The scientists knew lives and freedom were at stake—they decided they would need to secretly test the plutonium bomb before attempting to use it in warfare.

Both Einstein and Oppenheimer worked at Princeton's Institute for Advanced Study in 1950.

Oppenheimer chose an area 210 miles (338 km) south of Los Alamos and called the test site "Trinity." He set up observation bunkers 10,000 yards (9,144 m) away from ground zero to collect data, such as how much energy the explosion created. The scientists didn't know what would happen. Fermi wondered if "the bomb would ignite the atmosphere, and if so, whether it would merely destroy New

DID YOU KNOW? Hollywood actress Hedy Lamarr applied her mathematics knowledge to co-invent a frequency-hopping spread-spectrum technique as an unbreakable secret code later used by the military.

Hedy Lamarr in the 1949 film Samson and Delilah *(left); a mushroom cloud created by an atomic weapon test (above).*

Mexico or destroy the world." Oppenheimer bet $10 it wouldn't even work. On July 16, 1945, in the desolate New Mexican desert, the first atomic bomb exploded. With a force equal to an almost 20,000-ton (18,144 t) dynamite explosion, the plutonium bomb was detonated from a 100-foot (30 m) tower. Scientists calculated the temperature at the center of the blast was three times hotter than the surface of the sun.

Germany had already admitted defeat by the time the atomic bomb was tested, but Japan was still at war. President Harry S. Truman and the Allies considered invading Japan. Generals estimated an invasion would cause between half a million to a million U.S. and Allied forces deaths. After much debate, Truman decided he would use the atomic bomb—the most powerful and lethal weapon humans had ever wielded.

In an official letter to Japan (known as the "Potsdam Declaration") dated July 26, 1945, Truman and the Allies warned that, if Japan did not surrender, its country would face "complete and utter destruction." The Japanese government never responded to the letter. The Allies found out from Japan's secret codes that the Japanese intended to fight to the death. Truman gave his official approval to unleash the bomb, writing, "Release when ready."

On August 6, 1945, with four scientists aboard the B-29 American bomber nicknamed the *Enola Gay*, the first atomic bomb made of uranium fell on Hiroshima, Japan. The resulting mushroom cloud rose an estimated 50,000 feet (15,240 m) and leveled almost 70 percent of the city, killing some 70,000 to 80,000. A second atomic bomb made of even more powerful plutonium was dropped on Nagasaki three days later. The Japanese did not know these were the only two atomic bombs the Allies had built. Emperor Hirohito cast the deciding vote among his generals for Japan to surrender

on August 15, 1945. The agreement was signed on September 2. In this way, applied science helped end a war. But at what cost? Critics have pointed out that science also helped destroy thousands of lives in the process. Oppenheimer publicly regretted his involvement and quoted Hindu scripture before the Trinity testing: "Now I am become Death, the destroyer of worlds."

Nuclear energy is controversial to some because of its usage in World War II and the arms race that followed. However, many scientists say nuclear energy could be the answer to current and future energy needs. Today, it provides about 12 percent of the world's electricity. Nuclear energy is used for radiation treatments in hospitals to fight off cancer. It is found in X-rays, microwave ovens, and other devices. Applied scientists are asking questions and making discoveries every day to find other helpful ways to use nuclear energy.

Scientists with the International Thermonuclear Experimental Reactor project aim to demonstrate the capabilities of nuclear fusion.

TRY IT OUT! Redesign an item to be ergonomic! Ergonomics is the science of making environments and tools more comfortable to increase productivity without injury. Think of something you use a lot and add or take away a feature to improve it!

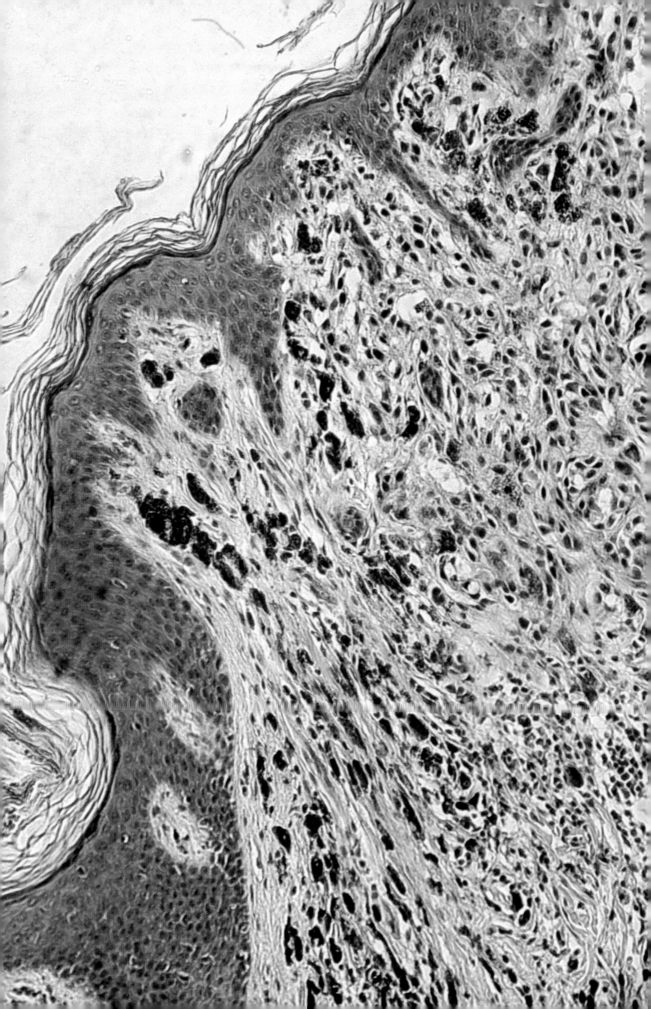

WORK IT, APPLIED SCIENTIST

CANCER IS A SCARY WORD. MANY OF US HAVE HEARD of or know someone who has had one type of cancer or another. It's a disease that starts at the cellular level. Cells are the smallest units that make up all living things. When cells are cancerous, they spread quickly and can build up into tumors. The body sometimes destroys cancer cells on its own, but when it cannot, the cancerous cells may move to other parts of the body and make the person sick.

Scientists from every branch of science apply their knowledge, ask questions, hypothesize, and experiment to find cures for cancer. American geneticist Mary-Claire King knew she wanted to fight cancer since she was 15, when she witnessed a friend die from a kidney tumor. King completed her bachelor's in mathematics by age 19

Beneath a microscope, clusters of tumor cells can be detected in a patient.

and went on to pursue a doctorate in genetics. Her doctoral **dissertation** is

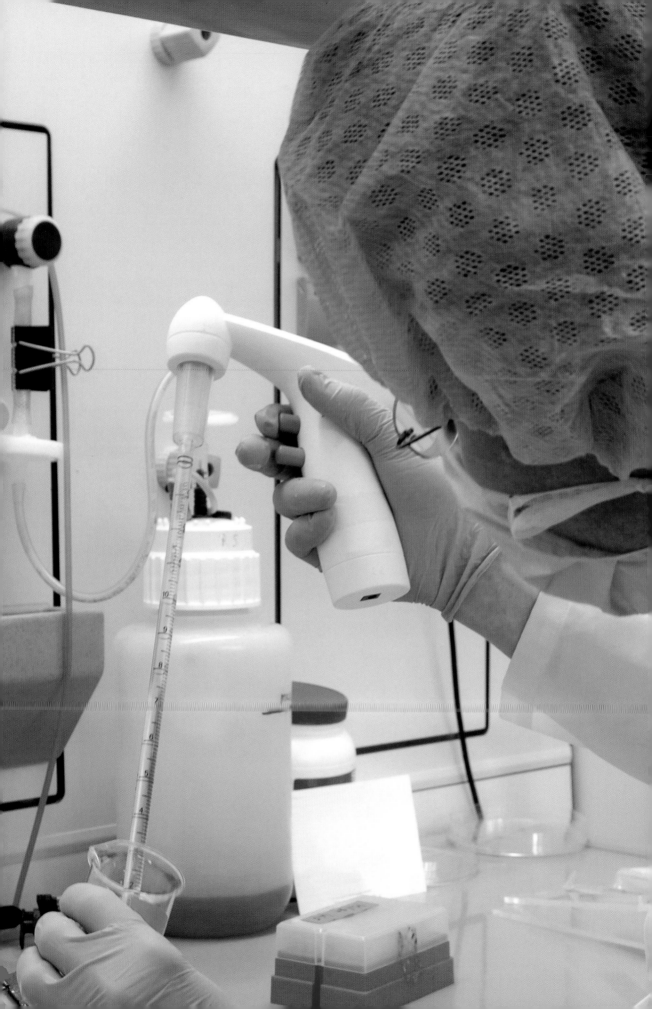

credited with revolutionizing the field of evolutionary biology. King compared human with chimpanzee proteins to prove that the two species share 99 percent of **genomes**. Scientists say this means that chimpanzees and humans split off from a common ancestor 5 million rather than 10 million years ago, as was once believed. Using her knowledge of the sciences and genetics, King applied it to cancer research. She hypothesized breast cancer had a hereditary link, meaning it could be passed from parent to child. She began studying DNA in families. Other scientists did not agree and criticized her hypothesis. However, after many years of detailed research and testing, King and her team of scientists found a **marker** on chromosome 17 in 1990.

Four years later, other scientists isolated the cancer-causing gene BRCA1. This has helped diagnose the 5 to 10 percent of breast cancer cases that are hereditary. From her own research on BRCA1, King was able to develop cancer testing and treatments. She had one patent (issued in 1997 for genetic markers for breast, ovarian, and prostate cancer), with others pending as of 2014.

King also took her hereditary science knowledge and applied it to help victims of war and human rights abuse. During Argentina's civil war in the 1970s, children were kidnapped and their mothers killed. Political leaders of the South American country later prevented grandparents of the kidnapping victims from claiming the children—unless they could prove their relationship. King developed a blood test for the grandparents using gene markers and DNA that could match them with their grandchildren with a greater than 99 percent accuracy rate. Her work for the United Nations War Crimes Tribunal has helped reunite more than 50 families.

King once said, "I think there are two keys to being creatively productive. One is not being daunted by one's fear of failure. The second is sheer perseverance." Even as she continued studying

Much of Mary-Claire King's (below) career has been spent testing genetic materials in labs.

NIKOLA TESLA

Born during a Serbian lightning storm on July 10, 1856, Nikola Tesla grew up to become famous for his electricity inventions. His electrical engineering career began at a Budapest telephone company and continued at the Continental Edison Company in Paris. He invented an electric motor using alternating currents—which was so different from the direct-current electricity then in use that no one wanted to invest in the idea. When Tesla moved to New York to work for Thomas Edison in 1884, he had only four cents and a flying machine sketch in his pocket. The two inventors soon butted heads, and after Tesla resigned, engineer George Westinghouse licensed his alternating-current patents. Invented in 1891, the Tesla coil is still used in electronic equipment such as televisions and radios. Before his death in 1943, Tesla had more than 700 patents worldwide and many more inventions he never bothered registering.

cancer, she also began mapping the gene for genetic deafness in attempts to clone it, which may lead to cures for hearing impairment. Much of King's research involves exploring how environmental factors can affect or interact with genetic **predisposition** to diseases or conditions. This is the case with her observations of HIV-infected patients as well. King looks for ways in which the disease is different from person to person, a method that may lead to better treatments or even wipe out the illness in certain populations.

Like King, aerospace engineer Burt Rutan sees problems or challenges as opportunities to create innovative solutions and improve the way humans live. It takes a persevering mind unafraid of failure to also engineer a plane that can fly nonstop around the world—or to design and build a spaceship.

First developed for the American navy, the F-4 Phantom II was also used by the marines and air force.

Newsweek magazine has billed Rutan as "the man responsible for more innovations in modern aviation than any living engineer." Since age eight, Burt showed an interest in aircraft, designing and building model planes. Both he and his brother Dick flew solo by age 16. Burt graduated near the top of his class at California Polytechnic State University with a degree in aeronautical engineering. Dick went on to more advanced pilot training as a fighter pilot in the U.S. Air Force. Burt worked for the air force as a civilian engineer on flight test projects for seven years. He gathered data on several different military aircraft such as the F-4 Phantom II Fighter, putting it through tests such as spins. He began asking questions and hypothesizing: What if a small airplane had a canard (a small wing) placed forward on the body similar to fighter planes? How would it affect the plane's **lift** if the airplane were light? How could it be designed to use as little fuel as possible?

N328KF

DID YOU KNOW? A unit of magnetic field strength and an American electric car company were both named after famous inventor Nikola Tesla.

A computer rendering of SpaceShipOne reentering Earth's atmosphere (above); a Tesla roadster in 2011 (left).

The VariViggen was Burt's first aircraft design, which he started building in his garage in 1968. Since he didn't have a wind tunnel, he attached a scaled-down model of the plane to the top of his car and measured aerodynamic forces as he drove along roads at varying speeds. In 1974, he founded the Rutan Aircraft Factory and in 1982 opened Scaled Composites, which designed and built experimental aircraft. Over the course of his career, Burt designed more than 300 aircraft—45 of which have flown.

One day while at lunch with Dick and fellow pilot Jeana Yeager, Burt drew the first design for a new aircraft on the back of a napkin. Five years later, on December 23, 1986, the Rutan Voyager, piloted by Dick and Jeana, broke the flight endurance record. Made of the lightweight composite materials graphite and fiberglass, Voyager was able to hold in its 17 tanks more than 7,000 pounds (3.2 t) of fuel. It had traveled nonstop around the world without refueling in 9 days, 3 minutes, and 44 seconds.

Eventually, Burt turned his focus to space flight. He wanted to create the first privately built spaceship the world had ever seen, and he achieved that goal with SpaceShipOne in 2004. The craft won the $10-million Ansari XPrize, an award offered to the team that could build a spaceship capable of carrying at least 3 people to an altitude of 62 miles (100 km)—accomplishing that feat twice within 2 weeks. "We proved it can be done," said Rutan, "by a small company operating with limited resources and a few dozen dedicated employees.... Space tourism will be a multibillion-dollar business." Burt was among *Time* magazine's "100 Most Influential People in the World" in 2005 and retired from Scaled Composites in 2011.

As Rutan has left his mark on innovative aircraft, so has computer scientist Ruzena Bajcsy in robotics. Bajcsy received master's and doctoral degrees in electrical engineering and a PhD in computer

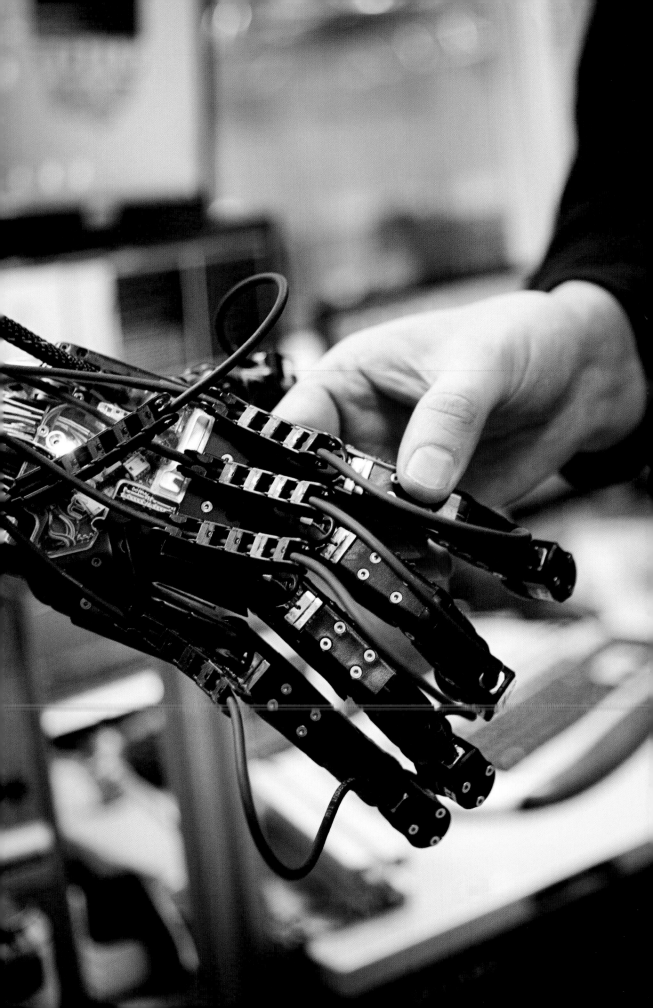

science. Since 1979, Dr. Bajcsy has helped create robots that can perceive their environment, respond to it, and communicate. She works on computer sensors in robotic machines capable of monitoring anything from forest fires to emergency 911 calls. "Many people think of robotics as mechanical things," says Bajcsy, "but robotics is also perception—and communication between machines."

A robotic hand's ability to perceive the type of object it encounters will determine its motion and reaction.

As of 2014, Bajcsy was a professor of electrical engineering and computer science at the University of California, Berkeley. Besides robotics, her many research topics included artificial intelligence (computers and machines behaving like humans) and computer vision (using computers to produce information from images and data). Engineers such as Bajcsy in the 21st century are rapidly applying scientific knowledge to technology. They are solving the issues of today and looking for the answers to tomorrow's dilemmas as well.

TRY IT OUT! Make a fruit battery: Gather an orange, 2-inch (5.1 cm) copper nail, 2-inch zinc nail, small LED light bulb, and copper wire. Poke the nails into opposite sides of the orange. Wrap a piece of copper wire around each nail head and the base of the light bulb. Watch the bulb light up!

ENGINEERING THE FUTURE

THE U.S. CENSUS BUREAU ESTIMATES THE WORLD'S human population to be more than 7 billion. With an ever-growing population, there are corresponding housing, food, and transportation demands. Some scientists think that because the ocean takes up 71 percent of our planet, the answer to our future housing needs might lie beneath the waters. Of the vast expanse of ocean, only 5 percent of it has yet been explored. Ocean resources may also provide cures for some of our diseases.

To live beneath the ocean for extended periods of time requires innovative engineering. There are a lot of obstacles to overcome. How will the person breathe in their underwater habitat? What construction materials are the best and longest-lasting? With such questions come hypotheses, testing, and observations. There is already one underwater

Observing animals such as sea lions gives scientists insight into ocean ecosystems.

hotel in the U.S. off the Florida Keys, with several more planned in other places such as the Red Sea near Dubai, Saudi Arabia.

Jules' Undersea Lodge sits 21 feet (6.4 m) below the ocean's surface in Key Largo. It was first used as an underwater research facility by aquanaut scientists studying the **continental shelf** along the coast of Puerto Rico. Former U.S. Naval Academy professor Dr. Neil Monney and aquanaut Ian Koblick co-developed the underwater dwelling in the 1970s and named it after Jules Verne, the author of the novel *Twenty Thousand Leagues under the Sea.*

The underwater habitat is filled with compressed air, which keeps the ocean water from coming inside the rooms. Scuba-diving guests enter as though coming up from the bottom of a little swimming pool. A cable delivers communications, water, electricity, and oxygen from the shore, and the underwater habitat is watched over at all times and has backup systems in place. Those who wish to mimic such structures visit Jules' Undersea Lodge for inspiration. "We have been approached by developers from around the world," says Dr. Monney. "To live beneath the sea was once just the dream of science fiction writers ... Now it is a reality. Here is a new step for mankind, the advent of undersea living, the taming of the last frontier on Earth ... Inner Space."

Jules' Undersea Lodge (opposite) was constructed decades after the death of namesake author Jules Verne (above).

In 2005, the Hilton Maldives' all-glass underwater restaurant Ithaa opened on Rangali Island, Maldives (now part of the Conrad Maldives Rangali Island). Up to 12 diners could enter the restaurant through an enclosed spiral staircase. But it had been more difficult to put together than engineers had thought it would be. Many times, the engineers had to make recalculations on the $5-million project. They had to keep checking the underwater building's structural balance and weight distributions. Then they had to make allowances

LEONARDO DA VINCI

The Italian Leonardo da Vinci (1452–1519) was one of history's most famous **polymaths**. Known for paintings such as the *Mona Lisa*, he was also an inventor and engineer credited with ground-breaking innovations such as the strut bridge, rolling mill, and lens-grinding machine. Some of his inventions were ahead of his time or too costly to build, but he wrote everything down, anyway. His journals contain inventions, medical drawings of dissections, architecture, designs for flying machines (400 years before the Wright brothers flew theirs), and war machines. A design for a diving suit meant to sabotage enemy ships was recreated by modern scuba divers, who found the wooden breathing tube and floating cork worked as an air device. Da Vinci never published his notebooks (written mostly in mirror-image cursive, which requires a mirror for other people to read it), and yet his fame spread throughout Europe and has endured across the centuries.

for the rising and falling of the tides. If those engineers experienced such difficulty on a relatively small structure 16 feet (5 m) below sea level, then the larger underwater habitats planned for future construction may encounter even greater obstacles.

On June 1, 2014, 6 marine scientists embarked on a 31-day stay in the underwater laboratory Aquarius. Located 63 feet (19 m) below the sea in the Florida Keys National Marine Sanctuary, Aquarius is a "habitat module" linked to a life support buoy. Oceanographer Fabien Cousteau, grandson of famous ocean explorer Jacques Cousteau, led the expedition (called Mission 31) and broke his grandfather's record of living underwater while performing numerous science experiments. "I couldn't imagine a better house than one under sea," said the younger Cousteau. He hoped streaming the expedition online and connecting to the outside world through Twitter and Instagram would help spark interest in marine discovery. Mission research projects included studying human sleep and the effects of **climate change** on ocean life, as well as testing underwater motorcycles and robots.

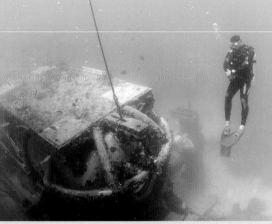

Researchers from Florida International University accompanied Cousteau to Aquarius in 2014.

Some robots in Hawaii have been used in response to concerns about overfishing. They have tracked the size and populations of fish in several locations. Armed with this data, the National Oceanic and Atmospheric Administration (NOAA) can make accurate fish catch limits or designate some parts of the ocean as no-fishing areas. Researchers are not only trying to preserve our fish supply, but they are also looking into how to harvest minerals and energy from the ocean without disturbing delicate ecosystems.

In addition to the oceans, applied scientists have considered the air above us as potential territory in which human life could expand.

DID YOU KNOW? The F-15 Eagle began flying in 1972 and is still one of the fastest airplanes in the

With more humans on the planet, there is greater competition for transportation. Traffic on some roads can be lined up for miles. What if cars could fly and avoid such problems altogether?

Terrafugia is a private American company headed by Carl Dietrich developing aircraft with foldable wings that can drive on roads. Engineer Burt Rutan also designed and built a hybrid gasoline-electric flying car. The Model 367 "BiPod" can build up enough speed to take off without the use of its four-engine-run propellers. The pilot/driver gets into the left side of the cockpit to drive. To fly, he climbs into the right side. When driven as a car, it can go 820 miles (1,320 km) on gas or 35 miles (56 km) on battery power. Once everyday automobiles take flight, some think the next logical step is to live in outer space.

At a distance of 238,855 miles (384,400 km) from Earth, the moon is the closest heavenly body to us, and we have landed our spacecraft on it. To enable living on the moon, though, there are many problems to overcome—not the least of which is the matter of food supply. The National Aeronautics and Space Administration (NASA) has experimented with **hydroponic** farming on space missions for more than 20 years. This kind of farming would not only provide fresh fruits and vegetables for the astronauts, but it would also help address another problem of living on the moon: the continuous need for oxygen.

Corporations are banking that engineers and scientists will be able to apply solutions for making space tourism a reality soon. Richard Branson's company, Virgin, has developed and built the Virgin Galactic space plane based on Rutan's SpaceShipOne. Advance tickets are on sale for $250,000 a person. Hilton Hotels has hired scientists and engineers to design accommodations on the moon that would be comparable to what people can find on Earth.

Even though there are still questions about practical issues such as where to live, scientists say the technology exists to at least transport us around. The Space Exploration Vehicle (SEV), which came from the earlier concept of the Lunar Electric Rover (LER), is one of the modes of transportation NASA has been developing that allows astronauts to get around on the surface of the moon. The SEV has 12 wheels that can turn a full circle and move in any direction. About the size of a pickup truck, the SEV can support two astronauts for up to two weeks. When the astronauts want to go outside to explore the moon's surface, they would wear spacesuits. Japan is investing 200 billion yen ($2.2 billion in U.S. dollars) to have a lunar science station at the moon's South Pole by 2020.

The success of unmanned Martian rovers such as Curiosity (opposite) helps NASA plan for the SEV (above).

The Boeing airplane company has its engineers applying their scientific knowledge for a space plane to taxi people into Earth's orbit by 2016. To encourage further lunar technology, Google started the Lunar XPrize. Google will award $30 million to the first privately funded organization that can land a robot safely on the moon. Some set their sights past the moon and seek to **colonize** the planet Mars. With a long history of applied scientists working on problems that once seemed impossible to solve, years of human innovation appear to prove that "where there is a will, there is a way."

TRY IT OUT! Draw sketches in a journal of a plant or animal and write your thoughts and observations. Take a cue from da Vinci and try to form some of your words by writing them while looking at a mirror.

climate change: a change in global climate patterns, largely attributed to increased levels of carbon dioxide in the atmosphere

colonize: to send settlers to an area to live

continental shelf: an area of shallow seabed located next to land

dissertation: a long written paper based on original research; it is often required for doctoral degrees

DNA fingerprinting: a method used to identify individuals by extracting samples of deoxyribonucleic acid (DNA) from body tissues

genomes: complete sets of genetic material located within living things

hydroponic: describing plants grown in water (or sometimes sand or gravel) but without soil

hypothesized: made an educated guess; suggested an explanation based on a limited amount of evidence

incandescent: glowing light produced from being heated by an electric current

lift: an upward force that works against gravity in a stream of air

marker: in genetics, a gene or DNA sequence whose location on a chromosome is known; it is used to identify a trait or a species

neutrons: particles without an electric charge that make up atoms

patent: a government-issued license that protects an invention from being copied by others

polymaths: experts in many subjects

predisposition: a tendency to have certain traits or conditions

protons: particles with a positive electric charge that make up atoms

scientific method: a step-by-step method of research that includes making observations, forming hypotheses, performing experiments, and analyzing results

Brinkley, Douglas, ed. *World War II*. New York: Times Books, 2003.

Burton, Walt, and Owen Findsen. *The Wright Brothers Legacy: Orville and Wilbur Wright and Their Aereoplanes*. New York: Harry N. Abrams, 2003.

Cheney, Margaret. *Tesla: Man Out of Time*. New York: Simon & Schuster, 2001.

Evans, Harold, with Gail Buckland and David Lefer. *They Made America: From the Steam Engine to the Search Engine; Two Centuries of Innovators*. New York: Little, Brown, 2004.

Harrison, Ian. *The Book of Inventions*. Washington, D.C.: National Geographic Society, 2004.

Kelly, Cynthia C., ed. *The Manhattan Project: The Birth of the Atomic Bomb in the Words of Its Creators, Eyewitnesses, and Historians*. New York: Black Dog & Leventhal, 2007.

Lester, Toby. *Da Vinci's Ghost: Genius, Obsessions, and How Leonardo Created the World in His Own Image*. New York: Free Press, 2012.

Yount, Lisa. *A to Z of Women in Science and Math*. New York: Facts On File, 1999.

NATIONAL GEOGRAPHIC: FINDING THE LOST DA VINCI
http://www.nationalgeographic.com/explorers/projects/lost-da-vinci/
This website has history on Leonardo da Vinci's creations and the quest to find his lost works.

PBS: TESLA, MASTER OF LIGHTNING
http://www.pbs.org/tesla/index.html
This website contains a visual biography of the inventor Nikola Tesla and interviews of experts.

Note: Every effort has been made to ensure that the websites listed above are suitable for children, that they have educational value, and that they contain no inappropriate material. However, because of the nature of the Internet, it is impossible to guarantee that these sites will remain active indefinitely or that their contents will not be altered.